Irish Sea Mossing in
Scituate Mass 1960-1997

Knee deep in Seaweed

Hawk Hickok Hickman

Hawk Hickok Hickman

Hawk Hickok Hickman has written four books. His other three books are-

"Hawk and Red Fox-Modern Day Gypsies" Volumes 1 and 2

and

"Seaweed Shanty Town", the prequel to this book.

'his book is primarily dedicated to Lucien ousseau Sr., who purchased our Sea Moss om us for most of our careers, and set an xample of hard work and it's rewards that spired us all.
is also dedicated to all the mossers of is time period and those who came before em. We were unable to contact or remem-r you all, but you are part of this book.

(Cover Picture-Retired mossers preparing for ossing reenactment in 2010, at Scituate Town Pier.)

Acknowledgements

Photographs– Bobby Steverman, Bobby Chessia, Ken Soderholm, Frankie "The Phantom" Jackson, Jerry Pallotta, Billy "Stets" Stetson, Lucien Rousseau Jr., Gary McEachern, Bobby Caggiano

Mossing Anecdotes– Bobby Steverman, Billy Stetson, Lucien Rousseau Jr., Bobby Francis, Jack Hoey, Gary McEachern, Jerry Pallotta, Bobby Caggiano, Kathie McDonald, Cindy Pallotta McEachern

Tow Boats– Pedlo Murphy, Bobby Steverman and Gary McEachern

(Graysole and Steel Boat)

(Bobby "Bopper" Gray)

Irish Sea Mossing in Scituate Mass

Knee deep in Seaweed

The Final Chapter
1960-1997

Tales of Irish Sea Mossing in Scituate Mass from the 1950's through the 1990's.

(The author, Hawk Hickman, mossing in Doherty's Cove between 1st and 2nd Cliffs)

Bill Sexton was a locally well known Scituate caricaturist and artist. Here we present his take on Irish Sea Mossing.

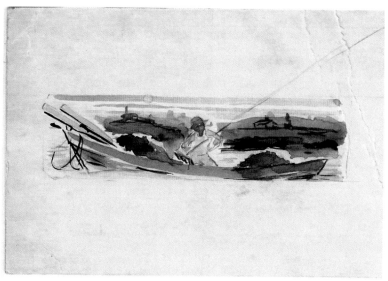

Prologue
3:30 A.M.–July 1960

I am in my parents' house in Scituate Massachusetts making peanut butter and jelly sandwiches. It is pitch black outside and about 58 degrees. I am dressed in a bathing suit with sweatpants pulled over it, sneakers and a sweatshirt.

I have packed water and fruit with the sandwiches. I have also packed insect repellant, sunscreen, sunglasses and a hat. I am 17 years old and so full of energy I feel like I might explode.

Why am I doing this and where am I going? I am an Irish Sea Mosser and this is part of my "kit". I will shortly be leaving the house (very quietly) and walking abo 100 yards to my dory, which is perched or the edge of the salt marsh, across the street.

I will carry my 14 foot sea moss rake , 8 foot oars, bailing bucket and thole pins the dory and , after placing all my kit an gear carefully in the dory, I will seat my

elf amidships and gently rock her off the
lge of the marsh, so that she slides grace-
lly into the water , which is about three feet
elow the
lge of the marsh.

lelight in this morning ritual (which will
ry in time as the low tide follows the phases
the moon). Hardly anyone else is up and
y immediate world is quiet and peaceful.
he dory slides off the marsh and the mo-
entum carries me towards the bridge con-
cting Second Cliff with the Scituate Har-
r downtown area and the harbor itself. A
v seagulls are aloft beginning their endless
arch for food and the sky begins to
tly lighten.

I take the first few oar strokes I give
nks for being alive and having an occupa-
that allows me independence of action
profitability based on my degree of ef-
. As I pass the inner harbor marinas and
roach the Town Pier area, I hear activi-
mongst the Lobstermen and Dragger

Fishermen Vessels still tied to their various moorings and piers.

My rowing strokes take on a more steady rhythm and I begin to inhale large quantities of wonderful New England salt air, air that Nantucket Whalers once inhaled as they prepared to sail far and wide.

I am careful to stay near the channel so as not to run aground. Every minute is valuable and time wasted by going aground can not be countenanced. Leaving the confines of the outer harbor, I decide on my course and destination.

Third Cliff it will be and hopefully I will arrive first and encounter flat calm seas and a bountiful crop. I am an Irish Sea Mosser and life rocks!!!!

INDEX

INDEX

Chapter 1-The Harborview

'he year was 1959 and we had just moved to
cituate. I was a junior in High School and
'as looking for a summer job at the end of
1e school year. I found one as a dishwasher
 the Harborview Restaurant (now known
; TK O'Malleys) True to its name, it sat
ght on Scituate Harbor and had a great
ew of the harbor.

 Occasionally,
taking a break
from the sti-
fling kitchen, I
would go out-
side to get
some fresh air.
On the harbor
would be vari-

; lobster boats, fishing draggers, gill-
ters, and leisure time power and sail boats.
thing unusual about this scene for a typi-
New England harbor.

13

What *was* somewhat unusual and caught more of my attention were the groups of smaller rowboats (which I later found out were dories) which would pass at certain times of the day, laden down with what seemed to be seaweed. Most of these were being rowed by young men of my age or thereabouts.

Intrigued, I began to make some inquiries amongst my acquaintances. Very quickly learned that these fellows were collecting Irish Sea Moss (Carrageenan) and following in the footsteps of Irish Immigrants who had brought the industry over from Ireland. Sea Moss contains an ingreent that serves as a food binder in the foo industry and

(Stafford Short and To Gray)

(Peter Hickman)

was therefore worth gathering.

I immediately sought out the buyer (Lucien Rousseau) and queried him on how one became a sea moss gatherer.

He explained that one had to wait for an available boat (or provide his own) and mossing rake. One then had to (if given a boat and a rake) prove that he was worthy of keeping the equipment by going out to sea every day and raking as much moss as possible at the going rate of 1.75 cents per lb..

(By the early 90's the price would be 10 cents) I was sold! I soon had a boat and rake and was ready to roll.

(Hawk Hickman-1960)

Lucien Rousseau was one of those larger than life characters and a somewhat intin dating personage when encountered for t first time. He was born in France, emigra ed to the US and served in the US Armed Forces.

When he first arrived, he spoke a lot of French and was soon nicknamed "Oui, oui", oui being French for "yes".

Lucien could just about fix and/or build any type of machine and then keep it rui ning forever.

He had a couple of old army trucks which he had rigged for loading and transporting he Moss and a loading tractor that was omething to behold.

Each day when we were through pulling our loads and had rowed them into the harbor, we would then wait for Oui, Oui to arrive with the mammoth tractor and truck.

Sometimes we would have to

ol our heels
r a while
nce he might
in the mid-
e of turning
d drying the
oss from the
evious day's
ul.

Scituate has four cliffs located right on the ocean, outside the harbor, and they run roughly from north to south, from the entrance to the harbor towards the mouth of the North River.

Peggotty Beach is located between Second and Third Cliffs and contained many summer homes back in th sixties.

In the earlier days of mossing (late 1800s to 1950s) there wer mossing shanties on Peggotty and som of the other beaches of Scituate. Many of the "old timers" would spend the be ter part of the summer at or around the shanties, drying and storing moss after

hey had brought it ashore. In more modern
imes (beginning in the late fifties), Lucien
would pick the moss up and dry it at his
and pit in Greenbush, on the Driftway,
current location of Scituate School buses,
ear Dunkin Donuts).

he Cliff Gang consisted of year round resi-
ents of the Cliffs and some summer resi-
ents. Most of these mossers, including this
uthor, kept their dories and skiffs in the
arbor, behind the bowling alley, in Cole
arkway (in the vicinity of the current Luci-
Rousseau Memorial Landing).

ere were sev-
al families
at had multi-
mossers ac-
e during this
e, including
Hickmans,
lottas,
inns, Shorts,

Caggianos, Grays and an occasional Archer and Borgatti. On a good day (sunny, gentle winds, cooperative tides) most of these eager young men could be seen racing out to the mossing grounds rowing or motoring

(Outboards had gradually crept in during the forties and fifties, but a few diehards st liked to row).

Irish Sea Moss grows on both sides of the North Atlantic and is generally found from the low tide mark out into deeper depths.

Rockweed and Kelp usually occupy the shallower areas between the high and low tide marks.

(A double string of dories leaving Scituate Harb

Ience the best time to rake the moss is from
:veral hours before low tide until several
ours after. Since low as well as high tide
.oves ahead each day, mossers go to work
 variable times.

1e Cliffs Gang was very
:gressive and competitive,
•th amongst its own ranks
.d with mossers from oth-
 areas of town.

(David Hickman)

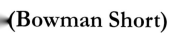
(Bowman Short)

(Tony Gray)

Chapter 4-The Sandhills Gang

Sandhills is located north of Scituate Harbor and it was from this area that we had another "mossing gang". Here there were the McCarthys, Timmy and Sean, Charlie Short, Joe and Steve Best, Paul McCarthy, Tommy McCarthy, Jack Hoey, Jim Kenny, John Salvadore, several Duffys, Dave Ball and a bunch of Pattersons including Tucker. Some of these were finishing up their mossing careers in the fifties and some were just starting in the early sixties

(Mike Duffy   (Chris Zucker
and Rick Franzen)   and Sean McCarthy

The McCarthys (Timmy and Sean) kept their dories on Jericho Beach in front of their father's house. Jericho Beach is in the Harbor, north of the Town Pier, just after the Scituate Yacht Club. Oftentimes we

ould see the Sandhills gang rowing out as
e rowed out from the other end of the har-
or. Usually they would head north along
e coast, up towards The Old Sow, Long
edge and Big and Little Jenkins, while we
ould head for the Cliffs.

A string of dories   (Tucker Patterson)
ntering the harbor)

during the tide, many of us would be
ncerned as to whether the other group
d found a better spot that day. There was
ense competition to see who could pull
most moss in any given tide and picking
right spot was very important.

(One of the Duffys preparing to
unload)

In and around the downtown Scituate Harbor area was another crew of stout lads, some of them with several generations of mossers in their ranks. Most notable amongst these may have been the Stetsons Billy and Bert Jr., the Stevermans (Bobby, Tommy, and Paul) and the Chessias (Bobb and Dickie). Others in the Harbor crew were Bobby Francis and Charlie Keyes. Some of these fellows would later move on to lobstering, gill netting, dragging and ot er types of fishing.

The Harbor gang would go either way wh leaving the harbor, either North or South. Everyone tried to guess the best spot to g each day. Wind direction played a big par in that decision.

(Bill "Stets" Stetson, Jack Du and one of Jack's sons)

Chapter 6 – Three Generations of Mossers

erhaps the most notable mossing family in
:ituate is the Stetson family. Billy Stetson re-
tes these remembrances of his time spent
aking sea moss". Here we paraphrase his

 story-
Billy started moss-
ing in 1956, at the
age of 16. Johnny
Bates, a legendary
mosser from the pri-
or era, showed Billy

: proverbial "ropes". Whatever John
owed Billy, it worked great, since Billy
uld get his rake in and out of the water
ter than anyone I have ever seen. If he
d been a gunfighter in the Old West he
uld have had the fastest draw. Billy went
to moss approximately 30 years out of the
t 41, winding up his career in 1997 at the
: of 57.
ly actually pulled and documented 20
ividual times when he pulled a ton or

more during his career, six times during the banner year of 1979 and three times at the age of 57, his last year-truly amazing statistics!

Billy's father, Bert Stetson, mossed from 191 to 1956 and also served on the Scituate Police Force for a good part of his life. In his retirement, he worked for Lucien Rousseau at the drying pit in Greenbush, drying, turning and baling the moss (middle picture on following page)

Billy's brother, Bert Jr. also mossed for a number of years.

Billy's grandfather, William Henry Stetson mossed during the late 1800s and into the early 1900's. And, William had married a Murphy, who had two prior generations of mossers on her side, so Billy can actually count five generations of mossers in his family.

(Pictures of 3 generations on the following page)

Billy Stetson in Cohasset Harbor)

(Billy Stetson's father, Bert Stetson Sr., baling moss in Greenbush)

(Billy Stetson's Grandfather, William Henry Stetson, with a load of moss)

Chapter 7-The Minot Ledge Gang

During the early sixties, we (the Cliff, Sandhills and Harbor Gangs) were so involved with our daily mossing activities that we weren't aware that there were other groups of mossers outside of our immediate area. Gradually we began to realize that there were other mossers down in the Plymouth/Kingston areas and up in the Minot/North Scituate area.

As we grew older and more adventurous, and as the moss in our area sometimes became thinned out as the season progressed, some of us decided to venture up to the ledges in the Minot area.

(The author mossing in the Minot Ledge area)

ince the Minot area was several miles from
ne harbor, we had to rely on outboards to
et back and forth. Some mossers even
noved their boats up to Cohasset Harbor,
hich was closer to the Minot area than
ituate Harbor.

nce we moved up there, we couldn't believe
hat we found! Instead of the good size
cks we were accustomed to, the ledges
re huge, continuous slabs of rock. This
ade the gathering easier, although some-
nes there was not as much shelter from the
nd as there was near the harbor. Our loads
gan to increase in size and we wondered
y we hadn't found out about this fabulous
a sooner (it had been kept somewhat of a
ret by the few North Scituate/Minot
ssers).

(Duncan Sparrell and
Gary McEachern unload-
ing in Cohasset)

Additionally, Lucien did not encourage ledge mossing because he had to haul the moss further to get it to his drying pit in Greenbush (Irish Sea Moss needs to be dried blac or bleached white in order to be useable/ saleable).

In any event we (the older guys with access to motors) prevailed upon Lucien to let us move to Minot. We left the younger mossers to "scratch" moss in the harbor area while w raked in the "goldmines" of Minot. For the next few years, we would start the year in th harbor and then move to Minot when the h bor area was "scratched" out.

(The Minot Gang-Gary McEachern, Jerry Pallotta, Rick Franzen, Frankie Jackson, Duncan Sparrell, Bobby Caggiano, David Hickman, Hawk Hickman)

rry Pallotta, the Alpha Big Dog of the
:ggotty gang, was the guy who first
;ggested going up to Minot and we were
rever thankful to him for his great idea
ventually one of his sisters would marry a
inot/North Scituate mosser,
ter McEachern).
lditionally, Peter's brother Gary would
irry one of Jerry's cousins, Jeannie Mazzo-
(more on these mossing romances later).

(Jerry Pallotta)*

thor's note: Jerry has since become a
l known writer of children's books, with the
yline of many of them being in the Atlantic
an area of the South Shore of Massachusetts.

Lucien had a competitor buyer in Kingston. Van Tangley Sea Moss Company bought moss from the mossers operating out of White Horse Beach, Ellisville and various other areas of Plymouth. Occasionally they even made forays up into Brant Rock in Marshfield. We became more aware of this crew as the years went by and invited them up for a rowing race at the end of one parti ular season.

Spirits were high on that day and a great ti was had by all. Later, after Lucien passed away, Paul Van Tangley would begin to buy moss in Scituate and thereby keep the indu try alive through the 1990s.

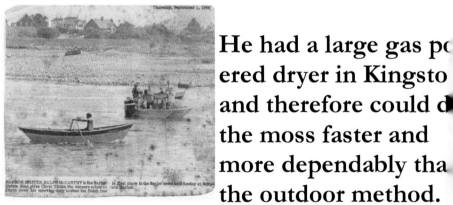

Thursday, September 1, 1966

HARBOR MASTER RALPH McCARTHY in the Harbor · in first place in the Senior event held Sunday at Scitu-
Police Boat gives Chris Tilden, the winners salute as ate Harbor.
Chris rows his mossing dory across the finish line

He had a large gas po ered dryer in Kingsto and therefore could d the moss faster and more dependably tha the outdoor method.

(Chris Tilden winning the dory race in 1966)

More Dory Race Pictures
(courtesy of Bobby Chessia)

(Dory Races continued)

(Gilman Wilder in checkered shirt, Murray Snow in baseball cap)

(Murray Snow, Gretchen Scarry (Dory Race Queen), Mrs. Chessia, Steven Caggiano, Dave Borghatti)

Chapter 9- The Sheriff

One of our most notable mossing buddies was nicknamed "The Sheriff". His real name was Tommy McDonough and he lived in Second Cliff. He was the nephew of the former and locally famous Governor's Counslor, Sonny McDonough.

Tommy was famous for coming out each day with a whole bunch of candy. He would have candy bars, tootsie rolls and all sorts of assorted goodies. We hardly ever saw him with regular food. He had a small lightweight boat and put in a summer or two in our ranks.

We were somewhat taken aback by his presence since he came from a well-to-do family and probably didn't really need to be trying to take on the difficult task of mossing. In any event we all liked him and welcomed him to our ranks.

Bobby and Steven Caggiano)

35

Chapter 10-Kenney and Hoey

In or around 1960, there appeared a very strange sight on the mossing scene. Now, we were used to some pretty strange sights so it took something really out of the ordinary to get our attention. That something was two young men showing up to moss o of the same boat! To the best of our knowledge this had never happened befor other than perhaps an older mosser show-ing a tyro the ropes for a few days. These guys, Jim Kenney and Jack Hoey, actually planned to go out together every day , mo together and share the profits.

Inwardly we were shaking our collective heads because we knew there was a reaso no one had ever done this. Two people in the same small dory or skiff would be cor tinually getting in each other's way. We d cided to keep our opinions to ourselves a: see what developed. They did manage to make it through an entire season albeit w much arguing and whacking of each oth body with rakes and oars. By the time th second season arrived, they decided they had enough money for a second boat and had enough of the mossing "togetherness". However, because of that one bizarre year mossing in the same boat, their names would be forever tied together as "Kenney and Hoey" within the mossing fraternity. As an aside, both Jim Kenney and Jack Hoey would continue mossing into the late sixties. After that, they both, as was the case with many mossers, "hung up their rakes" and moved on to more traditional work and raising families. Jack returned for a brief period in 1974 for the express purpose of writing a story on mossing for Yankee Magazine. Below are several pictures that appeared in that article, including one of Jack mossing.

(Jack Hoey)

(Joe and Jerry Pallotta)

Down on **Peggotty Beach** there was an enclave of **Italo-Americans** who had been summering at **Peggotty** for several generations. These families consisted mostly of **Pallottas, Quinns, Caggianos** and an occasional **Tamuelevitz**. The matriarch of the clan was affectionately called "Nana" by all of her various grandchildren, and many times would prepare large quantities of Italian food for her mossing brood.

She would brook no disobedience and whenever she called one of them they would come running, even if they were in the middle of a tide. Sometimes some of them would forget to take a lunch out and so, since they were usually mossing near her house, she would

ell to them at
unch time to
ome in and get
ome food. Matt
uinn, especial-
, who was her
vorite, loved her
ooking and would al-
ays come running
hen she called.
heir invariable reply,
lled across Peggotty
ove and reverberat-
g off Second and
ird Cliffs, was "Comin' Nana".

The person or persons being called would immediately scoot in for a quick meatball sandwich or some other delicious snack.

As we began to approach our 20s (and even older for some of us) even the ledges in Minot became regular fare. We began to lu for a bigger challenge. Someone suggested the Gloucester area since there were plenty of ledges there, and so began the makings of our great Gloucester Expedition.
Seven brave and hearty sailor/mossers signed on; Peter McEachern, Jerry Pallott: David Pallotta, Gary McEachern, Hawk Hickman, Gary Quinn and Bobby Caggia

Obviously we would need more horsepow overnight provisions and good planning. We eventually prevailed upon our two Nor Scituate/Minot buddies, Peter and Gary McEachern, who had a powerful lobster boat, to tow about eight of us up to Gloucester.

e waited for
ood weather,
acked our
eeping
ags, food,
d other
ar, and
ade way for
Gloucester, on a beautiful late
mmer day, sometime in the late seventies.

e trip, as you can imagine, took several
urs and by the time we arrived we did not
ve a lot of time for that afternoon's tide.
raked as much as possible before dusk
d then anchored the boats in Gloucester
arbor. Our plan was to get up early, hit the
rning low tide, add as much moss to our
ds as possible and steam back to Scituate
the afternoon.
eryone except me was up for going in to
ucester to party down. I was tired and
yed behind tending the charcoal stove.
ile they were gone, I fell asleep, the boat
rocked by a wake, the stove tipped over,

charcoal burned the deck and the stove wen overboard-not a good ship's watch for me! When my shipmates finally returned (they had been visiting a few bars in town), it was dark, so they didn't discover my negligence until the next day, and even then they were all so intent on pulling a good tide that it was placed on the back burner, so to speak. In the morning, I was the first up and decided to go on a scouting mission in my dory, even though it was too early to begin mossing. After rowing around the cove we were in, I thought I had spotted a possible good location. Way down in the water it looked like there might be a Moss covered ledge.

(Homer Winslow Painting of Gloucester Harb

readied the dory and lowered my rake
into the water. Down and down it went, the
full 14 foot length before I seemed to have a
hold on something. I had my hand on the
very end of the rake and had leaned over the
gunnels to get the rake even lower in the
water.

Slowly I pulled on the rake and my heart
sped up. The rake had that feel that only
occurs when it is pulling on some really
thick moss. I pulled the rake across the
unseen ledge and then rapidly pulled it up
into the dory. I could not believe my eyes! It
was one of the biggest rake fulls of moss I
had ever seen.

In a state of high excitement, I lowered the
rake again and had the same result! I could
not even see the ledge, but began to pull in
rake full after rake full. This was a mossers
dream-to find a spot no one else knew about
and get a jump on every-
one.

(Artist drawing by
Margherite Moore)

Slowly I became aware of activity on the lob
ster boat as the night owls began to awaken
They didn't notice that I was already at wor
and even when they did, I tried not to let or
to my discovery. By that time, I estimate I
had a good 300 to 400 pound head start,
which is a substantial amount.

Soon they had all joined me in the same ge
eral vicinity and each went to what he
thought would be a good area. To make a
long story short, we killed it that morning.
By the time the tide was over, we had all
filled our boats, which meant anywhere fro
1500 to 1800 pounds. We couldn't have bee
more pleased with our little Gloucester cov
find. As we made our way back to the lobs
boat and climbed on board, the grumbling
began. Where the hell was the charcoal gri

(Artist drawing by Margherite Moore)

erry Pallotta cooking burgers on exhaust pipe)

ter McEachern, Jerry Pallotta, Hawk Hickman
and Gary McEachern)

David Pallotta towing the seven skiffs back to
Scituate.)

I finally had to admit my screw-up. There ensued much yelling and ball busting, bu finally they let up as we tried to figure a way to cook our burgers and dogs. Finall we hit on a solution. Every lobster boat has a vertical exhaust pipe with a large fl surface on the top and it is red hot when the engine is running. We would cook on the exhaust pipe!

We cooked, ate, drank and steamed back to Scituate, arriving just before dusk. A band of modern day inshore mariners completing a wonderful adventure.

Lucien was waiting f us at the ramp and we unloaded boatload afte boatload of some of t cleanest moss he had ever seen. For one of th few times during unloa ing, he had a smile his face from ear to e

Chapter 13-Pedlo Murphy & the Cheap Bastard from Second Cliff

The Steverman clan had a maternal grandfather named William James Murphy whose nickname was Pedlo. Evidently one day he received a mailing on which he was addressed as Pedro.

The Post Office employees began calling him Pedlo and thus his nickname. Pedlo's main claim to fame was that he was the last person known to walk from 3rd Cliff to 4th Cliff before the great storm of 1898 broke through, creating a permanent separation now known as the mouth of the North River. (The old mouth was a few miles south at the northern border of Marshfield).

When I met Pedlo in the early sixties, he was one of those great salty old-timers who had a few lobster traps and would go out each day in his skiff and pull them. One day I happened to be rowing in from mossing as was my custom when he happened by on his way in.

He offered me a tow in and, not wanting to be rude, I accepted (I actually enjoyed my rows in and out each day). As Pedlo untied me when we had arrived in the inner harbo I offered him a small compensation to help him out with his gasoline bill. He took the money and putted off to his mooring.

I thought nothing more of it until his gran son, Bobby, told me that when Pedlo arrive home, he was muttering about that "cheap bastard from Second Cliff".

Evidently Pedlo thought we were all well-t do up on the Cliffs and that I should have dug down a little deeper into my wallet. H was a great old guy and I will always remember that story with fondness.

(Tommy Steverman a Pedlo Murphy)

Iere is Bobby Steverman's continuation of
his story, "On an early morning tide on third
iff, I asked my grandfather if I could
orrow his skiff with the outboard, knowing
at we would be back in the harbor before
:00am. He said 'okay, but don't tow more
an 3 dories and don't tow that, cheap bas-
rd from 2nd cliff'.

; we were coming back in around 11:00
had a string of 5 or so dories and at the tail
d was Hawk Hickman. My grandfather
is standing on the town pier pointing his
ager as if counting the dories. When we
me closer he saw the last dory and started
mping up and down. Hawk waved to him
d we all started laughing. That was the last
he I used his skiff."

(Pedlo Murphy on left, Pedlo with
Tommy Steverman on right)

Chapter 14-The Ton Club

In the mossing subculture of the 60s and 70 and on up to the 90s, it was a badge of hono if you could lay claim to having pulled a ton of moss in a single tide. Since the length of time in a tide suitable for pulling moss is about 4 hours, this means one has to pull 50 pounds per hour, while taking time out to b water out of the boat every so often.

Further complicating the task was that mos of the boats did not have a ton capacity anc even if they did, it became very difficult after 1500 pounds. The boat became fuller and fuller and lower in the water as the mosser tried to keep bailing , mossing and keeping the boat afloat.  (Bill Sexton drawir

The obvious solution was to bring two boa out, but it was difficult sometimes to judge when to take the extra boat.

n order to pull a ton, conditions have to be
lmost perfect. What you need is a full or
ew moon tide where the tide goes out con-
iderably further than a normal low tide.
hese are called minus tides and some can
e as much as two vertical feet lower than a
ormal low.

he second prerequisite is to have light
inds or no wind. Light or no wind causes
e ocean to be what we call "flat calm" and
ables the mosser to see through the water
the moss better.

hirdly, a spot where little or no mossing
s occurred that year up to that point helps
great deal. So ideal conditions, as de-
ribed above, coupled with having the fore-
ht to obtain and bring a second boat, give
e mosser a fighting chance. In spite of all
ese obstacles several mossers in our era
ulled a ton", some of them several times.
nongst them are the following; Billy Stet-
n, Jerry Pallotta, Matt Quinn, Lucien
usseau Jr., Sean McCarthy, Gary
Eachern and Peter McEachern.

As hard as it may be to imagine, Billy Stetson actually pulled over <u>three thousand pounds</u> in one tide. This would be like some one hitting six home runs in one nine innin game.

Billy listed his occupation in the annual Scituate Town Report as Mosser and rightfully so, as he probably mossed off and on for a good 40 years or more.
He continues working on the ocean at the writing of this book, stern man on a lobster boat skippered by another old mosser, Sean McCarthy.

("Stets")

Chapter 15- The 50,000 pound club

Another benchmark distinguishing a top notch mosser was the total amount of moss pulled in a season. If a mosser hit or went over 50,000 pounds that was considered an exceptional feat. We had several people who hit that mark in several different seasons. When one considers the fact that the season ran from roughly mid-June to mid-August, about 60 days, and that you would usually hit at least 10 days of really bad conditions, this meant that you had about 50 days to hit the mark.

That translates to an average of 1,000 pounds per tide. Not an easy task, but with our competitiveness and youthful energy we were able to do it. One of the mossers who attained this mark were Hawk Hickman, Jerry Pallotta, Lucien Rousseau Jr. and Billy "Stets" Stetson.

(A string of dories returning to Scituate)

(Mossing near Minot's Light
in Cohasset)

Chapter 16- 30 Days in a Row

_erry Pallotta and this author were two of
_he most competitive mossers during the
_ate sixties and seventies. We had to check
_ach day to see who had the most moss for
_he day and so far that summer. We became
_bsessed with the competition.

_ne summer it got so intense that we would
_oth go down to the ramp behind the bowl-
_ng alley and check the weather. If it was
_nywhere near decent, we would go out so
_hat neither of us would lose ground to the
_ther.

_ell, it got so bad that we would just go out
_o matter what the weather was like and
_hen watch the other one to see if he went
early. We went on like this for 30 consec-
_tive days, gradually losing weight until we
_ot only didn't have an ounce of fat on our
_dies, but began to look gaunt. Finally we
_nde a mutual agreement to take a day

off and rest. Resting never felt so good! We had each lost about 10 to 12 pounds and needed to rest and gain a few pounds back.

(The author mossing that summer)

(Jerry Pallotta that same summer.)

Chapter 17- Double Tides

s alluded to in an earlier chapter, a mosser
as to follow the tides as they vary from day
 day. He/she must be ready to get posi-
oned in a suitable area two hours before low
le and be prepared to pull moss until two
ours after low. This is when the beds of
oss are most accessible and during any
ne before or after that the mossers
ectiveness drops rather quickly.

hat to do then when the time of low tide
proaches 6 p.m.? It is at this point that the
osser has to decide if he wants to continue
ossing in the late afternoon into dusk or
n to the early morning low tide.

cisions would be made based on the
ather and cloudiness vs. sunshine. Windy,
udy or rainy weather in the afternoon, with
recast of clearing in the morning would
nt the mosser towards the following morn-
rather than that afternoon.

Occasionally some of the more ambitious mossers would opt to go out for both tides, gathering as much as they could in the after noon and then piling more in the boat the next morning.

This could lead to problems. One had to be very careful (if Lucien did not unload late i the day) to leave the boat where it would nc be aground in the morning.

Five hundred pounds or more gathered in the afternoon/evening tide could easily cause a boat that would normally be floatir freely to be hard aground, especially if the mosser was late getting up and the tide ha gone out further than the point at which it had been anchored.

This author's personal belief was that it wa more effective to just make a clean cut one day and move from afternoon tides to mor ing tides. Others believed in pulling "doubles" for everything they were worth.

You could get more moss this way more often than not, but usually wound up totally
exhausted after a couple of days of this.

two strings of dories and skiffs returning to
Situate Harbor in the early evening, under a full
moon. See story on following page about this picture).

Mossing skiffs and dories tied up in the Inner
Harbor, next to Cole Parkway)

The following story is about the best double tide ever, as related to the author by Jerry Pallotta-

"We left at 4am to go to the Minot Ledges. We saw the sun rise. It was full moon and flat calm. We unloaded around 1pm.

At 3pm we went back to the ledges, flat calm, great mossing, we all had big loads. We came in at dusk and as we approached the Scituate Harbor Jetty, it was dark and then the moon came up. What a fabulous day! Best ever! Two tides. We saw the sun rise, then saw the sun set and finally we saw the moon rise."

This is the kind of a day none of us who were there will ever forget , and why we loved mossing so much.

(Dories ready for unloading

Chapter 18– Beers in the Lobster Trap

There were some peripheral activities that weren't strictly related to mossing but utilized some of the mossing gear. Occasionally after mossing hard for a week or more, we would feel the need to blow off some steam.

That usually meant party time on Peggotty beach, in the evening. We would find someone to buy us some beer, pull our dories up on the beach in the evening, after unloading our moss, and get ready to "party down".

Since some of us were under 21 and since alcohol consumption on the beach was illegal, we had to be creative in order to enjoy a full night of drinking and carousing. We had grown tired of Scituate's finest arriving on the beach and confiscating our precious beer, so we hit upon a novel idea. We would take most of our beer down to one of the dories and row it out to a lobster pot.

We would then "haul" the pot and place the beer in the trap. One or two beers each would be returned to the beach to be consumed while waiting for the inevitable cruiser arrival. When the officers would approach us, we would quickly finish off whatever we possessed and watch them while they searched around for additional supplies.

(Peggotty Beach with 3rd Cliff in the Distance)

Eventually they would leave, scratching their heads in puzzlement and after a suitable w we would row out, haul the traps and bring more libations ashore. They never did figure out our scam and so we were able to drink and carouse as long as we didn't disturb the peace.

Chapter 19-Black Tom

With every unusual, offbeat occupation such as mossing was, there were the inevitable characters that were attracted to the activity. One of these was a fellow who was known as Black Tom. He was as Irish as they come and when we knew him in the late sixties, he was probably in his late fifties or early sixties.

We found out as time went on that he was a throwback. He was one of those guys who had mossed in the 30s and 40s and occasionally came out of the woodwork to pull a tide with us.

Tom always had a big smile and an endless stream of banter, much of which was unintelligible due to the speed with which his verbalizations sprung from his Irish mug. Tom also always seemed to have a minor buzz on and we strongly suspected he had some of the "Nectar of the Gods" in his very before, during and after the tide.

In any event, he was a wonderful addition to our band of mossing warriors and we always looked forward to his occasional appearances.

(Old time mossers spreading moss on Peggotty Beach)

(Frank Fallon and wife rinsing moss)

Chapter 20-Bailers and Girlfriends

One of the difficulties encountered during mossing is the accumulation of water on one's dory. Each rakefull of moss comes into your boat dripping with seawater. That water collects behind the "gate" in the stern of the boat.

Therefore, periodically, during the tide, it was incumbent upon the mosser to bail the water out. Failure to do this in a timely fashion could result in extreme difficulties, including swamping and sinking.

There were several ways to approach this issue. The first was to make time every so often to bail the water out yourself. The only drawback to this method was that every minute spent bailing was time you weren't pulling in moss.

The second and more preferable way was to enlist the aid of a young mosser "wannabe" who was chomping at the proverbial bit to go out with you for a tide.

These youngsters were usually in good sup-
ply and could often be enlisted for the chore.
They would usually be quite happy with a
couple of bucks for their efforts.

Finally, many of us had girlfriends who
could be cajoled into coming along to bail.
Quite often, if the weather was conducive,
they would use the time to work on their
tans, when not actually bailing. This usuall
involved a bikini and additionally they wou
make a lunch. This was the best of all
worlds and on those particular days "It jus
didn't get any better", as they say.

(The author ba
ing the dory on
the tow into the
harbor. Note
how low in the
water the dory

Chapter 21-Oilers

There were many tricks and techniques utilized by the mossing fraternity in the never ending quest to gather more moss. One such was the technique known as "oiling". Now before any current day environmentalsts get all bent out of shape, the oil to which we are referring was generally either Cod Liver Oil or vegetable oil. The idea was to "flatten" the surface of the water by applying some of this oil to the area being mossed.

This would enable the mosser to see through the water better and thereby gather more moss. Various methods were used in this endeavor, amongst which were spray bottles and floating oilers. Those with the spray bottles would spray oil on various rocks upwind from where they were mossing. The oil would then drip off the seaweed covered rock and slick down the area downwind from it. The mosser would position himself in the slick and start raking. The oilers worked the same way, onl they were floating on a little wooden frame with a lightweight anchor holding them in place. During the tide, new areas would need to be oiled and we would constantly b oiling new rocks and moving oilers to new positions.

Tony Gray mossing at Third Cliff
in "flat calm" conditions)

Chapter 22- Cindy Saves the lunch

One day Peter McEachern was mossing in Strawberry Cove in Cohasset and had brought his girlfriend, Cindy Pallotta, with him to bail (and make a lunch). It was a beautiful day for mossing and they soon had quite a load of moss.

Cindy, who was supposed to be bailing, became so entranced with her handsome boyfriend that she was not bailing as quickly as she should have.

Peter, who was concentrating intently on his mossing (with occasional furtive glances at Cindy in her bikini) did not notice how low his skiff was in the water.

All of a sudden an ocean swell carried them up onto a ledge so that the bow was up higher than the stern. Water quickly began coming in over the stern and they realized they were sinking. Peter, at that point, uttered the soon to be famous words, "Cindy, grab the lunch!".

In other words, in typical male fashion, the food was far more important than Cindy's safety. Eventually they were able to get the dory bailed out and return safely to the harbor, albeit with much less moss that they had at the moment of sinking.

(Gary and Peter McEachern)

(Peter McEachern)

Chapter 23-Irish Mossing -Rivalry and Romance.

(As told by Gary McEachern)

'Back in the mid 1970's I was mossing out of Cohasset Harbor and pulling some big loads. My brother Peter and I were competing with each other every day. One year Peter did not moss because he went offshore fishing, so there wasn't much competition for me.

Somehow Lucien figured out that I was very competitive. So just about every day Lucien would tell me that there was a guy in Scituate that was pulling more than me. I did not realize it at the time but Lucien was a master at motivating each mosser to pull more and become better and better.

With some kids he would tell them to work longer or faster, or he would say 'ya know the more ya pull, the more ya make'. He would tell some to go out even if the weather was not so great. But for me he would make it a competition, because he knew I hated to lose. I always wanted to be the top mosser.

Almost every day, after I weighed in, he would say I had pulled the most in Cohasset but there was a guy in Scituate beating me. After a while I became frustrated and just couldn't believe that someone was beating me almost every day.

I asked Lucien who this guy was and he said his name was Jerry Pallotta. He stated that Jerry had several brothers who were really good mossers also, and they could also beat me. So Lucien created a great rivalry between Jerry and me. In the process of creating the rivalry between us, he also created a rivalry between Cohasset and Scituate. This was how Lucien motivated everyone to do their best.

After a couple of weeks of getting beat almost every day, I suspected Lucien was pulling my leg. So I decided to see for myself if this guy was really beating me. I went to Scituate and from a distance watched them unload. I saw what Jerry weighed in at. The next day I asked Lucien if Jerry had beaten me, and of course the answer was yes. But I knew better!

The fact remained that Jerry and I were rivals, but I liked the competition. I decided to make a real competition out of it and I went to Scituate to meet Jerry and let him know what had been going on. Wouldn't you know, Lucien was telling Jerry that I was beating him, almost every day!

Jerry and I kept the competition going but it was on the up and up. We told each other what our weights were, and even though we were rivals, we soon became friends. I also became friends with Jerry's brothers and eventually I met the whole family- Jerry's parents, brothers and sisters.

Gary McEachern and Jerry, Allotta, first two on the left)

One day I was at Pallotta's beach house to compare loads with Jerry and his brother David. My brother Peter came along. Peter got to meet the whole family too. He met Jerry's sister Cindy.

It didn't take long; Peter was spending a lo of time at Pallotta's talking with the guys, and especially Cindy! After a little while Cindy was going mossing with Peter, she w supposed to be keeping the boat bailed.

To make a long story short, the romance be gan and still continues today. Peter and

Cindy were married in 1978. But here's the rest of story. It turns out that the Pallottas had a lot of cousins, and David Pallotta int duced me to one of them - Jeannie Mazzo

Soon another romance was born. It also co tinues today. Jeanne and I have been marri since 1980."

Chapter 24-The Greatest Show on Earth

One year we had an "Eager Beaver" show up at the unloading ramp asking the usual question, "How do I go about getting involved with this endeavor". This particular day I was the recipient of the inquiry and decided to really give him the reality of the situation.

His name was Kevin Corbett and he would go on in later life to become a Pediatrician. I looked him square in the eye and told him that getting into the mossing game was similar to running away and joining the circus, only you didn't have to run away.

I told him that you needed to hang around the unloading ramp just like you would have to hang around the circus. You would look for and volunteer for any task that needed doing.

At the circus, you might be trying to help feed the elephants. At the mossing ramp, you would be helping with the unloading, making friends and trying to see if there were any available boats. Well Kevin did just that, and soon came on board as a "mossing intern". Kevin was with us for a few years and then went on to his real career, but mossing, as with many of us, helped him to pay his tuitions and get his feet on the ground.

I see Kevin around from time to time and he usually breaks out in a grin as we recall the "circus" analogy.

(Bowman Short's "Scottie" sometimes helped us unload)

Chapter 25– The Beadles Expedition and the Flying Spark Plug

As told by Bobby Steverman-

A bunch of us went down to Beadles, the ossing was terrible. The moss was like annel moss. I had less than a barrel (500 ounds) Burt Stetson had towed us down d when it was time to go home his motor 4 cylinder Mercury) blew a spark plug. The ug whistled by my head like a bullet (I uld feel the buzz by my ear).

rt took the outboard boat in to Brant Rock see if he could get it repaired, leaving me start rowing back to Scituate with his dory tow (a good 7 or 8 miles). He promised to k me up when the outboard was fixed. I ved, towing his boat for 5 1/2 hours ! I ught I was going to die. I could barely ve my arms and the sunburn was some- ng to read about. Another misadventure h Bert !"

(Bobby Steverman motoring above,
getting a tow and not rowing below)

Chapter 26-Attack of the Evil Midgies

Every few weeks as the moon and the tides worked their way around the clock, we would find ourselves unloading our moss at dusk. If we were lucky, the wind would be blowing. Why, you may ask?

Well if the wind died out completely, a hoard of almost invisible midgies (no-see-ums) would rise up out of the salt marsh mud flats and descend on any warm blooded creature in the vicinity.

Midgies are very tiny, voracious, insects, so tiny you can barely see them as they start biting you. It does not matter if you're covered from head to foot with clothing, they will bite your ears, nose, eyelids, anywhere they find bare skin. They will quickly drive you to the point of hysteria, because no matter how many you kill, another few dozen will quickly take their place. On the worst night I remember, we had just finished unloading and were trying to tie our boats up and bring our gear to our cars. Most of us had bathing suits on with a sweatshirt.

We literally had to dive in the water and swim our gear ashore. As we swam, we had to keep submerging our heads to get relief from being bitten. Then we had to dash to our cars, stow our gear, and try to drive away as quickly as we could.

After that particular night, we no longer were in disbelief of herds of caribou jumping off cliffs in the northern parts of Canada and Alaska to escape giant mosquitos. We itched for hours afterwards.

Looking back now, the experience takes on a somewhat comical overtone, but at the time it wasn't one bit funny. We were literally swimming and running for what we thought were our lives!

Chapter 27-The Nightime Headlight Caper

In 1965, Bert Stetson came up with the novel idea of mossing at night using headlights mounted on a wooden frame. He and Bobby Steverman took some headlights off a junked car, mounted them on a wooden frame using vice grips, and attached the lights to some batteries, using jumper cables.

The idea was that they could go mossing more often by catching the alternate low tides at night, when the wind was usually much lighter and no one else was out.

Once they had the device constructed, they loaded it in one of their boats and off they went to 3rd Cliff, in the dark, using flashlights. By the time they got everything in the water after continually putting things together that kept falling off or coming loose, the tide was half over. Additionally, they were so tired the next morning that they were unable to go out on the daytime tide, which turned out to be a great tide, with calm wind and clear skies. Needless to say, this nighttime headlight caper was never tried again.

(Stafford Short)

(Bobby Steverman and grandson)

(Ronny Fallon sitting on a bale of moss)

Chapter 28-Bert and Bobby try a new unloading method
(story courtesy of Bobby Steverman)

n the late fifties and early sixties, unloading
as still accomplished using baskets or
reels. Since this was quite time consuming
small containers, many mossers trying to
nload at the same time) some people grew
uite impatient and sought alternate unload-
ng methods.

ne of the most bizarre of these was the
lea that Bert Stetson Jr. came up with. He
ecided to cut the top of his old Plymouth
pen with a torch and load the moss into the
ck seat, through the now open roof.

e solicited Bobby Steverman's assistance
d they soon had the old Plymouth loaded
with smelly sea moss and salt water resi-
e. Off they went to Fitt's Mill in Green-
sh, where they knew they could get the
r and its contents weighed.

Once they had the weight registered, they drove the car to Lucien's pit where they proceeded to unload the moss, using pitchforks and then their hands.

Then, back to Fitt's to get the weight of the car without the moss. This was all well and good, but the net result was that it took them longer than if they had just had patience and used the basket and/or creel method. Can't blame them for trying though!

(Tucker Patterson getting ready to pull a tide 2010)

Now, while all this was happening, other mossers were watching and they too were impatient. One of them, Jack Stark, decided he had an even better idea. He would fasten roller skates to the bottom of his dory and once he had pulled his tide of moss, would simply tie his dory to the bumper of his car, pull the boatfull of moss out of the water and then tow it on the roller skates to Fitt's!

Needless to say, he didn't even make it up the unloading ramp onto the parking lot, as his new invention weaved uncontrollably all over the ramp. As you can imagine, these two experiments were met with gales of laughter as both proved to be highly comical in their trial runs. There was never a dull moment on the Scituate Harbor unloading ramp.

(Paul McCarthy and Tommy Steverman)

Chapter 29-Thunder and Lightning

As you can well imagine, on certain days in the summer in New England, there ar severe thunder and lightning storms. These, of course, can be very dangerous to mossers in open boats, holding long mossing poles. However, like many othe dangerous occupations, mossing attract ed many "dare devils". These guys woul go out no matter what the forecast, if they thought they could grab some poundage before the weather hit.

On one such day, Joey Jaymes, this au thor, and several other intrepid souls we out having a pretty decent hauling day. But soon ominous clouds and distant thunder began to manifest themselves.

The air took on a chill and the wind be gan to pick up. However, since we were hauling moss in hand over fist, we hung in there for a bit longer than we should have. All of a sudden there was a terrib

oud clap of thunder and a bolt of lightning
struck right in front of Joe's boat, just miss-
ng his rake and actually causing the water
o sizzle.

That was enough for us. We pulled up our
rakes, bailed some water out and tied up for
the tow in. Soon the wind picked up to between 25 and 30 mph and we were taking in
some water over the sides of the dories. So,
we had to keep bailing while we were mo-
ring along.

Then, disaster, as Joe's beloved Evinrude
ran out of gas. He had more in a gas can,
but with the severe conditions and the
boats pitching so much, he had a devil of a
time refilling the tank.

Finally we got underway again and gradually the conditions improved. Soon we arrived safely back in the harbor and the danger was quickly forgotten. Another exciting
day on the "Bounding Main"!

Chapter 30-Joey Jaymes saves Jerry Pallotta at Harvey's Cove

Joey Jaymes was another mossing character (most mossers had very unique characters). Joe was a physical fitness fanatic and would go on to be a gym teacher after high school and college. Joe was most well known amongst the mossing fraternity as being closely bonded to his three H.P. Evinrude. He just loved that outboard and would fuss over it like a mother hen with her chicks.

One day Joe had motored up to the Minot area and was pulling a tide alongside some of the other regulars. The mossing was good and everyone was looking forward to a profitable day. It was, however, a day when there were occasional large swells. Now a swell is a wave that hasn't broken (no white water). Swells are not as dangerous as breaking waves. In any event, when you venture in too close to shore, swells turn into breaking waves and breaking

waves can wreak havoc with a dory laden down with a sizable load of sea moss. Jerry Pallotta made the mistake of getting in a little too close to shore and got hit by a breaker. His boat was overturned and he was pinned beneath it.

Bowman Short-
3rd Cliff)

oe jumped out of his boat and helped erry get out from under his boat. Then they oth uprighted the boat (very difficult) and nen bailed the water out, after pulling it out

into deeper water and making sure that Joe's boat didn't get carried in also. A very exciting afternoon!

ey Jaymes with his
isty Evinrude)

Chapter 31-David Dwyer Saves Bobby Francis

Lucien Rousseau Jr. tells this story about Bobby Francis-

"Bobby was mossing at Third Cliff one day and had about a half full dory. There were swells coming in and you needed to keep your dory pointed into the swells so that you would not take a "breaker" on broadside. Bobby neglected to do this and had a wave hit him broadside and turn his boat right over.

David Dwyer had to "rescue" Bobby and get him out of danger. This meant maneuvering his dory in amongst the periodic waves, helping Bobby to get his dory righted and then towing him out into deeper waters so that he was not in any more danger." Regretfully, Bobby lost most of the moss he had pulled to this point (this is a sad fact of life whenever one gets swamped or overturned).

Considering the fact that Bobby was the son of the Harbormaster, this was a very embarrassing day for him! Lucien Jr.'s sage words of advice are "Never turn your back on the waves and always keep your bow or stern pointed into the waves". Wise advice indeed!

(Lucien Jr. and Bobby Francis with loads of which they are very proud)
(1966?)

Lucien , Bobby Francis, hn Salvadore, Jamie cDonald, Jack Hoey)

Lucien Jr. 2012)

And now, as sometimes happens when many years pass and memories grow dim, we have the actual victim, Bobby Francis, relating his remembrance of this episode " If my memory serves me correctly, we were all hauling ass from 1st and 2nd cliff to beat a nasty squall line that was the local equivalent of a hurricane. I was mayb 2-3 ft. inshore of the line of dories racing for the south edge of the breakwater whe I got hit by a rogue wave and nasty roller. The weather was so foul that we could hardly maintain course never mind even see each other. I was tossed out of my dc ry and the boat, with moss, was tossed over my head. I went under to avoid the boat, came up on the other side, and grabbed the gunnel to hang on for dear life.

(Bobby Francis, second from left)

The sea was so violent it tore one of my sneakers off my feet. My choice was to beach the boat if I could find a sandy spot on that rocky shoreline, or attempt to walk the dory around the corner and into a semi -lee on the south edge entrance to the har- bor. I walked the boat around the corner and found a safer area.

My good friend Jimmy Kenny, the only one of us that had a motor to tow our string, cut loose the string, came as close as he dared, threw me a lifeline and towed me to safety. It was ugly. I don't remember David Dwyer being involved, nor third cliff. "

(Left to right-Jim Kenny, Lucien, Jack Hoey, Sean McCarthy and Hawk Hickman in 2010, at mossing reunion)

There were many "part time" mossers, fellows that would show up every so often, usually on optimal mossing days. They would last a year or two and then disappear back into the Scituate biosphere.

One such was Phil Carl. As related by Lucien Rousseau Jr., a few of us were out at Long Ledge on a fabulous early morning tide. Everybody was hauling moss in, hand over fist, under beautiful conditions, with visions of dollar bills dancing in their heads.

Right at dead low tide, the best time for mossing, we suddenly observed Phil rowing in to shore. We thought, "What in the world is he doing?"
We thought maybe he had broken his rake or wasn't feeling well. It turned out that he was hungry and since his house was right there at the beach in Sand Hills, he decid

to go home for breakfast right at the best time of the tide!. We were flabbergasted. None of we hardcore mossers would ever, even remotely, contemplate such a move. It was equivalent to a sacrilegious act. To leave a mossing area with, figuratively, dollars laying on the ocean floor, waiting to be raked up was beyond our comprehension. None of us who were there will ever forgot this event or the perpetrator's name. Phil will always live in mossing infamy.

Chapter 33-Comedy on the High Seas

There were many days when we would be totally amused by some occurrence during a day of mossing. Here are some of the funniest stories-

Weekend Warriors

We called many of the power boat owners weekend warriors because we could see that many of them were not used to boats and being out on the water. Our favorite story, and one which we saw repeated several times, involves the launching of pow boats on the very same ramp at which we usually unloaded our moss.

Weekends, of course, were the busiest for taking boats in and out of the water and there would always be a certain sense of urgency, since others were waiting to launch or pull out. We were sometimes there with 20 or more dories, waiting to u the ramp to unload. It's not surprising th that sometimes there would be accidents Most were fairly minor, but occasionally there would be a real knee slapper (for u not the victim). This would occur when a person would forget to set the emergency brake in the tow vehicle . The ramp was fairly steep, so the tow vehicle, boat and boat trailer would all head for the "deep six". Sometimes the driver would be able to run, hop in the vehicle and stop it before it submerged, but several times we saw a vehicle go in right up to its windows. Since this is salt water, the resultant damage was pretty bad.

Cut Loose!
One time Lucien Rousseau Jr. was towing a few boats in and one of the fellows being towed (Sherry Barry) decided they were going too slowly and untied the boat behind him (Skipper Clements). Poor Skipper never knew what hit him. One minute he had a sweet, easy ride in and the next minute he was cut loose to row his heavy load all the way in.

Waking up the wrong guy !
There was a family on First Cliff (The Youngs) who owned the Boatyard there.

They had 6 children, one of whom, Denis, was one of this author's best friends. Denis would go out mossing occasionally when not working at the boatyard, and we had arranged to go out at the crack of dawn one day in order to catch the early morning tide When Denis didn't come out of his house at the appointed time (4 a.m.), I wrestled with whether or not to go in and wake him up.
I finally decided to go in because I knew he wanted to go out. So, into the dark house I went and made my way to his room. I bega. shaking him roughly and was greeted with loud shout!
I was shaking one of his brothers (Ralph) and he did-

n't know what was going on! I finally rustled Denis up, but his family tells that story to this day.

The Earwig Caper

(as related by Lucien Rousseau Jr.)

Excerpt from Lucien Rousseau (Jr.) "Tales of misadventure"

It's 5:00 Am. I park at (then) Paul Hickman's house on 2nd cliff to pick him up for the tide. He comes to the front door and says 'be right there I have to get my gear at the back of the house'.

Five minutes later I get out of my car and hear thumping noises from the rear of the house. When I reach the scene, Paul is stamping on the remainder of at least 100 earwigs varying in size from small to enormous.
As he explained it, they had taken residence in his boots overnight and when he dumped them out, they headed for refuge in the house."

(Lucien Jr.)

The Great Dory Surfing Contest
(as related by the author)

"One summer a big Nor'easter came through right in the middle of mossing season. The surf was up for several days and we were totally aggravated and restless. So I had the big idea that we should take the dories out and go dory surfing. O course we knew nothing about dory surfing and the skill set required.

We had fun on the way out of the harbor, riding up and over the waves before they broke and so we were feeling upbeat and confident as we approached the surf at th Peggotty side of 2nd Cliff.

We watched the waves for a while like the surfboarders do to get the lay of the brea so to speak and then several of us said 'kowabunga' and took off rowing to bea the band. You may be able to guess the rest!

Total chaos and disaster. Out of control do-
ies slewing sideways and being broached
by the waves as we sped in towards shallow
water and huge boulders.

We somehow managed to pull the boats out
of the surf as subsequent waves tried to
permanently maim us. Another fabulous
time!!!!!!"

Mossing Snippets from Kathie McDonald

"Foggy mornings– lost off 1st beach when
we rowed & rowed and ended up back at
the same rock-you'd have to wait until 11am
- noon when the fog lifted– Steven Cag-
nano-who mossed just enough to take a
nap in it.

August-late night weigh in-row back to
Teggotty and catch a shooting star. Don't'
forget those fabulous tans-you guys were
the envy of the local Irish boys...even
Hawk, was tanned."

In 1979, there occurred a classic duel between two of the top mossers of this era, Gary McEachern of the Minot Ledge Gang and Billy the Kid "Stets" Stetson of the Harbor Gang . They had a mossing duel for the ages on some ledges off Cohasset, under conditions that were so ideal that most mossers had seldom, if ever, encountered them.

First of all, the tides were huge, both the high and low. This means that the tide goes way out and exposes thick heavy moss that is usually difficult to see. On a big low tide it comes much closer to the surface and sometimes right out of the water.

Secondly, there was no wind whatsoever and a fairly thick fog. It's much easier to moss in flat calm conditions because you don't get blown around and you can see the moss better.

Thirdly, they were at a spot no one else had been to so far that summer. Finally, and most importantly, they had brought an extra boat with them in case they "hit it big".

This duel began on July 11th, at Loden's Ledge. Mossing in a dreamlike state, with the fog enveloping them and a thick carpet of moss everywhere they looked, they worked as hard and as fast as they were able, since they knew they were in a special "zone".

On this first day, Gary jumped in the extra boat as soon as the first one was filled and pulled his heart out for the rest of the tide. His final total was 2600 plus pounds, the most he had ever pulled !

Billy, meanwhile , was hauling in 2340 in the boat! This is a very difficult task since the more you haul in, the deeper the boat sinks in the water, and the more often you need to stop to bail out the water. Both gun slingers unloaded and went home exhausted, but also eager to return the following day, since the weather forecast was the same, the tide would be just as low and the knew of two other nearby spots that were also untouched.

The next day, they arrived in the same general area ,and decided to go to Allen's Ledge and a nearby spot called "The Nuns", named for it's location just offshore from a convent retreat. Gary dropped Billy at Allen's and went in to The Nuns with the extra boat.

Again they found themselves in an unreal mossing zone. At or around low tide on the second day, Billy had filled his boat and so he went in to The Nuns to see if Gary was using the spare boat. Gary was dead tired and told Billy to take it. Billy quickly tied his full boat up and returned to Allen's, using up precious time to switch boats.

He soon resumed his smooth, swift raking and raked his heart out. He knew he was headed for a one tide total that few if any nossers had ever achieved. All too soon the tide had crept in to the point where raking was no longer possible.

Gary hauled in his last rakefull, started up his outboard, towing Billy's first boat behind him and went out to Allen's to fetch Billy. As he approached Billy in the second boat, he could not believe his eyes. Billy had filled the second boat! Gary exclaimed, "Bill, you have over 3000 pounds!" (Billy had 3120 pounds, an almost unbelievable total).

Just to put this in perspective, pulling 3120 pounds in a tide means that you are pulling 3120 pounds in approximately 4 hours and 15 minutes, Since 4 1/4 hours equals 255 minutes, you are pulling in 12 pounds per minute or 2/10 of a pound every second.

You do not stop except to bail. You are bent over, straining your lower back, you are holding a 14 to 16 foot rake and standing in a wooden boat with unsteady footing and encountering the normal ebb and flow of currents and waves. You are grabbing a swallow of water and a quick bite to eat occasionally and bailing out excess water every so often.

This is an incredible feat, comparable to some of the athletic feats that Jack La-Lanne accomplished during his career. This is approximately 500 pounds more than anyone else had ever pulled in a single tide during the period 1958 to 1998. A truly remarkable accomplishment!

The two day duel was over. Both mossers had seen mossing nirvana, both had the use of the extra boat on one of the two days, both had broken all their previous records, Gary was the king for one day and then Billy the Kid resumed the throne.

What a duel! This was a two day tide for the ages and neither mosser will ever forget it. We are proud to be able to present the story on these pages and record it for mossing posterity.

(July 1974)

(...ary McEachern with a ...h of moss-...Cohasset Har-...or 1974)

(...ill Stetson ...addling a ton ...to the ...ituate Har-...r ramp)

A few "Old Timey" pictures from the forties, courtesy of Bobby Chessia. Carl "Chub" Chessia is Bobby's dad.

(Carl "Chub" Chessia)   (This is either Peggotty or the beach between 1st and 2nd Cliffs)

(Frank Vinal, Lucien's Partner, documenting poundage with a young Carl Chessia looking on)
(On the right-Carl Chessia hefting a classic wooden handle mossing rake)

Epilogue

As I finish writing this, in March of 2013, Irish Sea Moss continues to be gathered in certain areas of the Maritime Provinces of Canada, most notably Nova Scotia. There was also an effort last year to restart the Scituate market, but it did not come to frution.

The reasons for this are many, but suffice it to say that various seaweeds with the necessary food binder properties can be gathered elsewhere at lower cost .

If Moss gathering ever returns to Scituate, this author believes it will have to be mechnized so as to allow the gatherer(s) the ability to collect more moss faster and with less effort.

I am saddened to come to that realization because mossing was such a unique and great job for youngsters, but in this day and age it is very difficult to sustain labor tensive occupations.

So, it is with a mixture of fond remembrance and sadness that I end this book o recollections. Fond remembrance for all the great times we had while we engaged in this "Labor of Love" and sadness that new generations of Scituate youth will no have the opportunity to enjoy this wonderful and fulfilling occupation.

We will go down to the sea no more. Ou day is gone, perhaps never to return. Bu oh what times we had!

About the Author

Hawk Hickok Hickman is a 73 year old father of 4 and grandfather of 6. He is currently in the seventh year of full-time RVing with his partner, Red Fox.(1/2/17) They travel the country each year with two motorcycles, two kayaks and two bicycles, following the warm weather and returning to the Scituate/Marshfield area each summer.

This is Hawk's first book.

They have a blog describing their travels at

harleyhawk43.wordpress.com

Hawk can be contacted at

harleyhawk43@gmail.com

(Note, the author's dory, shown below in front of Lowell's Boat Shop in Amesbury Mass., was built there in 1970 and was utilized for most of his mossing career. Lowell's , established in 1793, is the oldest active wooden boat building shop in the U.S.)

Go to -
http://www.lowellsboatshop.com
for more information.

Made in the USA
Middletown, DE
30 May 2019